GEOGRAPHY MATTERS IN
the
INCA
EMPIRE

Melanie Waldron

heinemann
raintree

Edited by Helen Cox Cannons and Jennifer Besel
Designed by Philippa Jenkins
Original illustrations © Capstone Global Library Limited 2015
Illustrated by HL Studios, Witney, Oxon
Picture research by Jo Miller
Production by Helen McCreath
Originated by Capstone Global Library Ltd

Library of Congress Cataloging-in-Publication Data
Waldron, Melanie.
  Geography matters in the Inca empire / Melanie Waldron.
      pages cm.—(Geography matters in ancient civilizations)
  Includes bibliographical references and index.
  ISBN 978-1-4846-0965-1 (hb)—ISBN 978-1-4846-0970-5 (pb)—ISBN 978-1-4846-0980-4 (ebook) 1. Peru—Historical geography—Juvenile literature. 2. Human geography—Peru—Juvenile literature. 3. Incas—Social life and customs—Juvenile literature. 4. Peru—Civilization—Indian influences—Juvenile literature. I. Title.
  F3429.W28 2015
  985—dc23   2014013386

This book has been officially leveled by using the F&P Text Level Gradient™ Leveling System.

Acknowledgments
We would like to thank the following for permission to reproduce photographs: Alamy: DBA Images, 28, Mark Green, 19; Bloomberg via Getty Images: Andrew Harrer, 35; Bridgeman Art Library/Giraudon, 29; Corbis, 37, Alison Wright, 27, Bettmann/Philip Gendreau, 22, Broooklyn Museum, 30, JAI/Amar Grover, 38, National Geographic Society/Herbert M. Herget, 21, National Geographic Society/Kip Ross, 13; Getty Images/AFP/Eitan Abramovich, 40; Newscom: akg-images/Aurlia Frey, 17, Danita Delimont Photography/Peter Langer, 15, Getty Images/AFP/Jaime Razuri, 7, Robert Harding/Michael DeFreitas, 8, Robert Harding/Peter Groenendijk, 24, Robert Harding/Robert Francis, 23, ZUMA Press/Hughes Herv, 16; Shutterstock: AridOcean, relief map (throughout), casadaphoto, cover, Chris Howey, 32, Dr. Morley Read, 11, KBF Media, 4, Martchan, 34, Mircea Simu, 41, Vadim Petrakov, 5; SuperStock: National Geographic/Mike Theiss, 12; UIG via Getty Images: Werner Forman, 32. Design Elements: Nova Development Corporation, clip art (throughout).

We would like to thank Brian S. Bauer, Professor of Anthropology at the University of Illinois, Chicago, for his invaluable help in the preparation of this book.

Contents

Who Were the Incas? 4

Where Was the Inca Empire? 8

How Did the Incas Farm the Land? 12

What Were Travel, Transportation, and Trade
   Like in the Inca Empire? 18

What Were Inca Towns and Cities Like? 24

What Was Inca Life Like? 30

How Did the Inca Empire Come
   to an End? 36

Was Geography Important
   in the Inca Empire? 40

Quiz... 42

Glossary 44

Find Out More... 46

Index.. 48

Some words are shown in bold, **like this**. You can find
out what they mean by looking in the glossary.

Who Were the Incas?

From around 1400 to 1532, the Incas ruled over a huge **empire** that ran up the west coast of South America. Their empire was very well organized, and it had strong leaders and a powerful army. It became the largest empire in South America.

The area ruled by the Incas covered a wide range of landscapes, from sandy beaches to snow-capped mountains. Over six million people lived in this varied land, with over 100 different **cultures**. The strength of Inca rule managed to hold these different landscapes and cultures together in one huge empire.

Many Inca towns, such as Machu Picchu, were built on small areas of flat land in the mountainous landscape.

DID YOU KNOW?

The Incas were not the only ancient **civilization** to develop in South America. Before them, several other civilizations had existed. The Chavin civilization lasted from 1500 BCE to 300 BCE, in the mountains of Peru. The Nazca civilization lasted from 200 BCE to 600 CE, along the coastal desert areas of southern Peru. The Mochica (100 CE to 800 CE) lived in northern parts of Peru, and the Chimu (900 CE to 1430) lived in northern desert coastal areas.

Around 200 BCE, well before the Inca civilization, people created lines and patterns in the landscape. They did this by moving stones from the surface of bare, rocky, sandy areas. These huge shapes are called Nazca lines.

How did geography affect the Incas?

The geography of the Inca Empire affected many aspects of Inca life. The mountains influenced how Incas traveled, farmed, and lived. The climate was different across the empire, and it had an effect on the crops that the Incas could grow. The empire was shaped by the geography of South America, especially the long line of high mountains, called the Andes, that runs through the **continent**.

Who lived in the area before the Incas?

The Andes are the mountains that run down the length of the western side of South America. People began to settle in the Andes around 12,000 years ago. By around 2000 BCE, many groups had settled in the river **valleys** that stretched from the Andes toward the Pacific Ocean. This was the easiest land to farm, since it was flatter.

How did the Inca civilization begin?

Around 1300, the people living in the valley of Cuzco began to grow and gain power. Over time, they began to conquer other nearby groups, and the Inca state was begun. They called their state *Tahuantinsusy*—meaning "the land of the four quarters." The word *inca* in Quechua, the language of the Incas, means "ruler." The first people to use the word *Inca* to describe the whole civilization were the Spanish invaders who ended the civilization.

At first, the Incas did not set out to conquer more distant lands. For around 100 years, they controlled quite a small area near Cuzco. However, in the 1400s, this changed. After Pachacuti became the leader around 1438, the Incas set out to conquer neighboring groups and to increase the size of the empire dramatically.

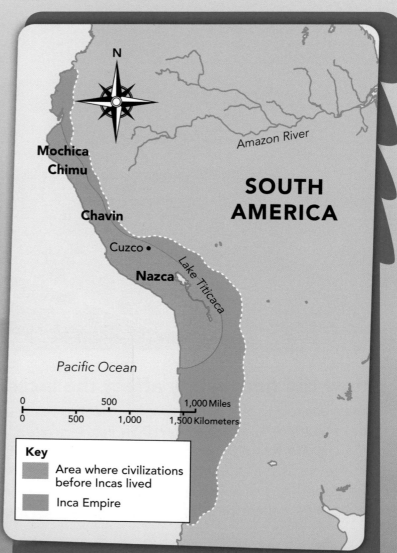

This map shows where the early civilizations, before the Incas, were located. None of them managed to gain control over such a large area as the Incas did.

HOW DO WE KNOW ABOUT THE INCAS?

The Incas did not use writing, so there are no records written by them about their life. They used different ways to record information—for example, stories, songs, and poems. However, **archaeologists** and historians have discovered lots about Inca life. They have examined Inca ruins and the tools, cloth, pottery, and even bodies that they found there. These things have given us many clues about Inca life.

This is an Inca **mummy** that was found, frozen in ice, at the top of a volcano. Archaeologists have studied the body to find clues about Inca life.

Where Was the Inca Empire?

At its largest, the Inca Empire stretched for about 3,000 miles (4,800 kilometers) along the western side of South America. It was narrow, only reaching about 200 miles (320 kilometers) inland from the coast to the jungles of the Amazon. It ranged from sea level to the high mountains of the Andes and included varied **terrain**.

What was the geography of the empire like?

As is true today, a vast desert ran up the length of the coast. It is dry and **barren**, and there is very little life there. The land rises up into the **foothills** of the Andes and the mountains themselves. The mountains are steep and rocky, with high **plains** and valleys between them. To the east of the Andes are areas of tropical rain forest, with lots of rivers that drain eastward into the mighty Amazon River.

Life for Incas in the coastal deserts was very different from life in the Andes mountains, and they had to find different ways to farm the land.

DID YOU KNOW?

There were sometimes long periods of drought in the Inca Empire, when very little rain fell. This would affect farming and food supplies. However, Incas were skilled at storing food for long periods of time, so they usually managed to avoid starvation.

This is a physical map of South America. The Inca Empire is to the left of the dotted white line.

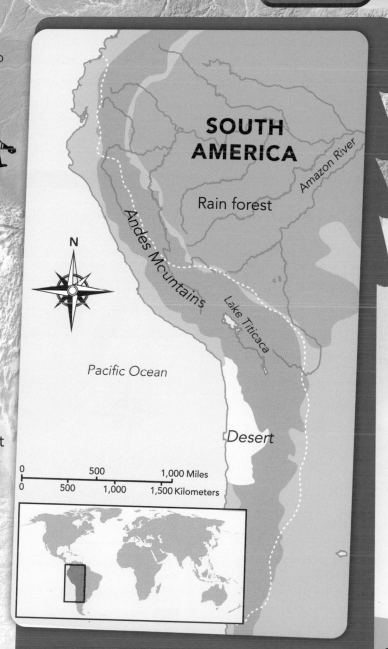

SOUTH AMERICA

Amazon River

Rain forest

Andes Mountains

Lake Titicaca

N

Pacific Ocean

Desert

| 0 | 500 | 1,000 Miles |
| 0 | 500 | 1,000 | 1,500 Kilometers |

What was the climate like?

The climate was as varied as the landscape. The deserts were hot and dry, but cold at night. The rain forest areas were hot and **humid**. Up in the mountains, it could be warm in the daytime and freezing at night. There were often snowstorms and hailstorms as well as high winds. The rainy season was from December to March.

How did the Inca Empire become so large?

Starting around 1300, the Incas began to expand and settle into the areas surrounding the Cuzco Valley. Then, in 1438, the Inca ruler Pachacuti took the empire to another level. He was a good soldier and leader, and he began a huge campaign to gain new land for his empire. He was helped by the rugged landscape of the Andes. Many groups of people lived in small valleys, cut off from other groups. This meant that they could not join together to fight back against the Incas.

The Inca army grew bigger. Pachacuti and his son, Topa Inca, pushed the empire northward. After Pachacuti died, Topa Inca continued conquering land to the south, and the next leader, Huayna Capac, gained a bit more land in the north. In addition to the land they conquered and the **minerals** it contained, the Incas wanted to be in charge of the people and their herds of animals. Taxes demanded from the conquered peoples would provide money for the Incas.

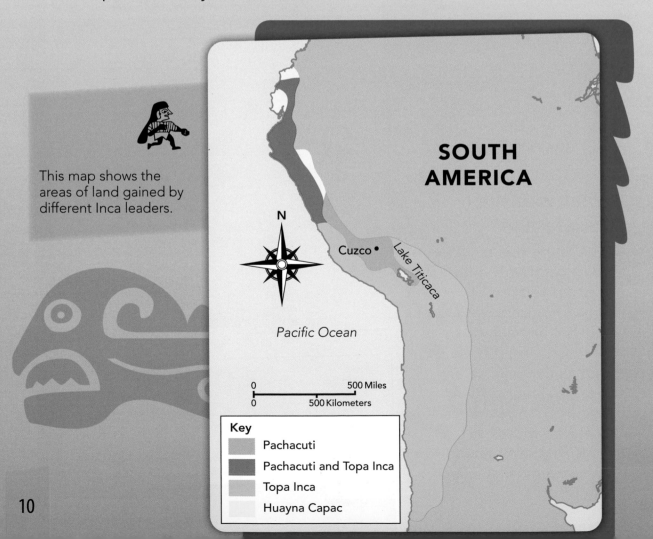

This map shows the areas of land gained by different Inca leaders.

SOUTH AMERICA

N

Cuzco •

Lake Titicaca

Pacific Ocean

| 0 | | 500 Miles |
| 0 | | 500 Kilometers |

Key

Pachacuti

Pachacuti and Topa Inca

Topa Inca

Huayna Capac

WHY DIDN'T THE INCA EMPIRE GO FURTHER INTO THE RAIN FOREST?

Topa Inca invaded the rain forest to the east of Inca lands. However, he was defeated by groups there. The Incas did not have much experience with living and fighting in the rain forest. They were unable to move easily through land covered in thick forest with many large trees. The Incas had to cut their way through bushes and **vines** and cross rivers.

How Did the Incas Farm the Land?

Much of the land in the Inca Empire was difficult to farm. The deserts were too dry, with **infertile** soil. The mountains were too steep, and the rain forests were covered with trees. The high, flat plains were often dry and very windy. However, the Incas used their skills to make the most of their land and to farm successfully. Land was farmed by groups of families, which ensured that everyone had enough food.

Seabirds like cormorants provided the Incas with valuable fertilizer for their farmland. Even today, cormorant poop is a highly prized item.

DID YOU KNOW?

The Incas figured out that they needed to keep their soils healthy, if they were to keep growing crops on them. They used **fertilizer** to keep the soils **fertile**. Animal and human manure was used for this. Nearer the coast, guano (bird poop) was used as fertilizer, since there were many seabirds.

How did the Incas farm on steep slopes?

Rain falling on the steep mountain slopes would simply wash the soil down the hill. The Incas had a clever solution. They built **terraces** into the mountainsides and strengthened them with stone blocks. All of this was done by hand. These terraces made great steps of flat land, about the height of a person, up the sides of mountains. They stopped the soil from being washed away.

In addition to building the stone walls of the terraces, Inca people had to bring countless baskets of soil up from the valleys to fill the terraces. The soil had to be deep enough for crops to grow. Underneath the soil, each terrace had a layer of gravel to help water drain properly through the soil.

Incas built terraces on the steep slopes so they could use them for farming.

How did the Incas water their crops?

Incas built systems to capture and channel water. In areas with very little rain, they built **reservoirs** to collect any rain that fell. They also built channels from wetter areas, or nearby mountain streams, to run into these reservoirs. A different set of channels would take water from these reservoirs to the fields and terraces that needed it.

Inca engineers occasionally changed the course of rivers. They straightened some rivers, to improve the flow of water and to stop the water from **eroding** the precious flat land in the river valleys. They diverted streams to flow in new directions. They used stone blocks to change the shapes of rivers and to form the sides of new channels.

Incas used their knowledge of rivers and the landscape to create channels like this one.

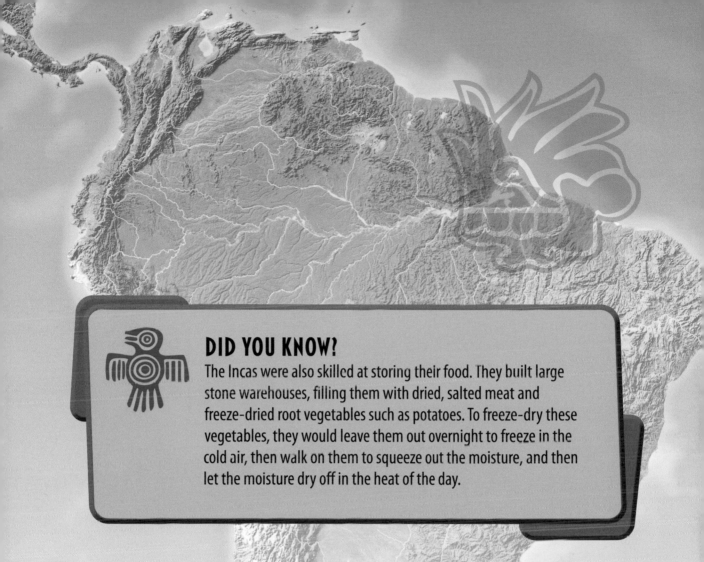

DID YOU KNOW?

The Incas were also skilled at storing their food. They built large stone warehouses, filling them with dried, salted meat and freeze-dried root vegetables such as potatoes. To freeze-dry these vegetables, they would leave them out overnight to freeze in the cold air, then walk on them to squeeze out the moisture, and then let the moisture dry off in the heat of the day.

What made the Incas such successful farmers?

When the Incas conquered new areas, they took seeds from other places in the empire to grow there. They took seeds from newly conquered areas and spread them in other places. They also moved farmers around, to spread their knowledge about growing certain plants.

Some terraces stepped up mountains for more than 3,280 feet (1,000 meters). This meant that crops were grown under varying conditions. For example, crops at the top of the mountain would be in much colder temperatures than crops at the bottom. This gave the Incas a range of plants that could cope with different environments, and so again guarded against food shortages.

What crops did the Incas grow?

Potatoes were first grown in South America. The Incas grew over 200 different kinds of potatoes. Some kinds were particularly good at growing in the thin mountain soils.

A tough grain crop called quinoa grew very well in the high plains of the Inca Empire, even those over 12,500 feet (3,800 meters). It coped with the warm days and freezing nights, and the Incas boiled the grain to make a kind of porridge.

In the lower valleys, the Incas grew corn, cotton, and beans. In the lower, tropical areas, the warmer temperatures meant that they could grow nuts, fruits, and vegetables such as avocados, chilies, and tomatoes.

Quinoa was very well suited to growing in the high plains, and the Incas made good use of this crop.

Llamas, alpacas, and vicuñas were highly prized for their wool and as pack animals.

DID YOU KNOW?
Only the oldest llamas would be killed for their meat. Incas did not have cows, pigs, sheep, goats, hens, or turkeys. Instead, they often ate the meat of guinea pigs, which they kept in their houses.

What animals did the Incas raise?

In the high grasslands and plains, Incas raised herds of llamas, alpacas, and vicuñas. Some families had very large herds of animals, and the families tagged the ears of their animals to show who owned them. Alpaca wool was spun to make fine clothes, and the wool from vicuñas made the finest-quality clothes for important people. Coarser wool was made into everyday clothes, sacks, and ropes. Llamas were also used as pack animals to carry loads and for their meat.

What Were Travel, Transportation, and Trade Like in the Inca Empire?

Even though the Inca Empire was huge, and the terrain was difficult, the Incas managed to build an amazing network of roads and bridges. This meant that people, goods, and messages could move quickly and efficiently around the empire.

What were Inca roads like?

The Incas built two main roads that ran the length of the empire. One was up in the mountains, and the other was along the coast. A network of other roads linked towns and villages to these main roads. There were over 15,000 miles (24,000 kilometers) of roads in total.

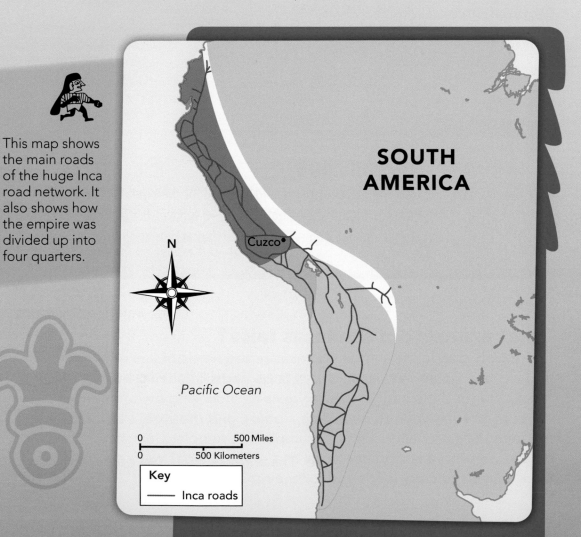

This map shows the main roads of the huge Inca road network. It also shows how the empire was divided up into four quarters.

SOUTH AMERICA

N

Cuzco

Pacific Ocean

0   500 Miles
0   500 Kilometers

Key
—— Inca roads

Some Inca bridges were over 200 feet (60 meters) long. They were narrow, and people could not pass each other.

Where the ground was marshy, the Incas built stone paths that were higher than the marsh. Some mountain roads had hundreds of stone steps to help the travelers up the steep slopes. Roads in the deserts were lined with tall posts to help guide people in sandstorms. Many roads were paved with the stones that the Incas quarried, making them smooth to travel on. Inca leaders chose people to work as road monitors, keeping the roads clean and clear.

How did the Incas build bridges?

Inca roads had many bridges crossing rivers and **gorges**. Stone towers were built on either side of bridge crossings. Ropes were fastened to these towers and then slung across to the other side and secured there. These ropes then had other ropes braided between them, to form a walkway.

How did the Incas travel?

There were no wheeled vehicles or horses in the Inca Empire. This meant that everything had to be carried on foot or on the backs of llamas. Some rivers did not have bridges built across them. Instead, people and goods were pulled across in baskets. The baskets hung from ropes that were attached across the river or gorge. People could rest on long journeys at rest houses called *tambos*.

Inca **nobles** were often carried on seats on **litters**. These would need a number of men to lift them. On rivers, lakes, and the sea, people sailed on rafts made of reeds.

DID YOU KNOW?
Llamas could not carry very heavy loads. If the loads were too heavy, llamas would simply sit down and refuse to move. They were also quite slow, only managing around 12 miles (20 kilometers) each day.

How did the Incas communicate?

Messages from around the empire had to be sent to and from the capital city of Cuzco and other towns. Messengers would run between staging posts on the roads, and messages from the coast could reach Cuzco high in the mountains in only six days. If there was an emergency, fire beacons were lit all the way to Cuzco. An army would be sent immediately in the direction of the beacons, to meet up with the messenger and hear the news.

DID YOU KNOW?

Inca messengers, known as *chasquis*, would memorize and then repeat their messages to another messenger at the next staging post. They would blow on a conch shell to warn the next messenger to get ready. By passing the messages along like this, a message could travel up to 200 miles (320 kilometers) a day.

 Llamas were valuable pack animals. This artist's painting shows how they would look carrying cloth and pottery.

What items did the Incas trade?

The Incas did not use money. Instead, they exchanged goods for other goods. People living in the mountains would bring wool, potatoes, and llama meat to markets. They would trade these for goods such as fish, cotton, and fruits that people from coastal areas brought. Incas from jungle areas would trade birds, rubber, and wood. People from all over the empire brought cloth, carvings, and pottery to trade at markets. The government controlled trade in luxury items such as gems and feathers.

Incas would bring items like this ceramic pot to trade at markets.

Why was trade limited in the Inca Empire?

There was not a huge amount of trading that took place in the Inca Empire, compared with some other civilizations. Farmland was shared among family groups, and some land was kept aside for the Sapa Inca—the Inca leader—and his family and for the temples of the Sun God that Inca people worshipped.

This is an Inca Sun temple. Incas had to give a lot of what they harvested to temples like this.

All men over the age of 25 had to do some work on the Sapa Inca and Sun God land, as part of a **labor tax**. In addition, families were not allowed to keep and trade everything they grew—only about one-third of it. One-third was given to the Sapa Inca, and the final third was given to the temples of the Sun God. This meant that families had very little left over to trade.

DID YOU KNOW?

The labor tax that Inca people had to pay was called *mit'a*. In addition to working on farmland belonging to the Sapa Inca and the Sun God, they had to help with building projects. They also had to serve in the Inca army.

What Were Inca Towns and Cities Like?

The Incas were talented **architects**, engineers, and builders. In addition to constructing the network of roads and bridges, they built some amazing buildings in and around their towns and cities.

What construction methods did Incas use?

Very skilled stonemasons would cut stones from the quarries in the empire with incredible accuracy, so that the stones were the right size and shape. Some buildings were made from very regular blocks of stone. Others were made from irregular blocks. These would be cut and shaped precisely so that they would fit together perfectly. The stones were cut so accurately that they did not need **mortar** between them to hold them together.

Many Inca buildings were built using stones carved to fit together like a jigsaw puzzle.

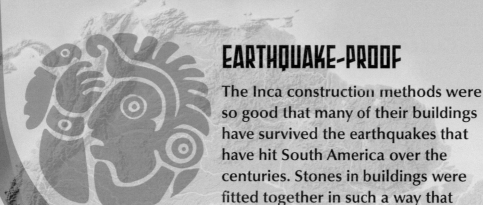

EARTHQUAKE-PROOF

The Inca construction methods were so good that many of their buildings have survived the earthquakes that have hit South America over the centuries. Stones in buildings were fitted together in such a way that allowed them to move during an earthquake and then settle back into position afterward.

DID YOU KNOW?

The Incas used stone hammers to chip blocks of stone into precise shapes. Blocks were then lifted into place, some weighing over 20 tons. The shaped blocks fitted together so perfectly that not even a knife could be slipped between them.

What materials did builders use?

Large and important buildings were planned out using models of clay. Then they were built using stone blocks such as granite. A stone or wooden beam would sit above doorways, and the roofs were made of **thatch**. The thatch would sit on top of a wooden frame that was tied onto stone pegs at the tops of walls. People built their houses using **adobe** bricks. These were made from clay and dried in the sun.

Building stones were dug out of quarries. Large blocks were moved using ropes and wooden poles that the blocks were rolled over. The Incas built ramps so they could roll the blocks up to the correct level.

What was Cuzco like?

Cuzco was the capital of the Inca Empire. Cuzco means "navel" (belly button) in the Inca language. The city was built near the place where the four quarters of the empire met. Around 80,000 people lived in Cuzco. The city was enclosed by mountains and sat at an **altitude** 10,500 feet (3,200 meters) above sea level. There were two rivers, Huatanay and Tullamayo, flowing through it.

Cuzco was the religious center of the Inca world, as well as the place where the empire was run from. There was an open square in the center of the city and a Sun temple nearby. The Sapa Inca and Inca nobles lived in buildings around the square. There was a huge **fortress** called Sacsayhuaman that stood on the high ground overlooking Cuzco. This fortress defended Cuzco from attacks by other groups.

Cuzco is based on a grid layout. The four roads heading out of the town led to the four quarters of the Inca Empire.

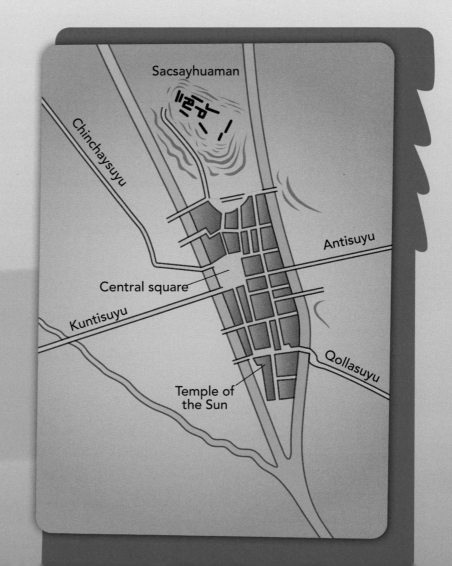

Sacsayhuaman

Chinchaysuyu

Antisuyu

Central square

Kuntisuyu

Qollasuyu

Temple of the Sun

Inca villages were perched high up in valleys on rocky outcrops of land. These are the ruins of Huinay Huayna.

What were Inca villages like?

In mountainous areas, many villages were made up of small houses built around a central village square. Houses were small, often with just one room. They were made with stone walls and thatched roofs. There would be an area for a fire in a corner, and since there were no chimneys, the smoke would simply rise up through the thatch. Many villages were built on rocky ledges rather than on the precious, flat farmland.

On the flatter land near the coast, houses were made of adobe bricks and were painted in bright colors. Near forested areas, houses were built out of wood.

What was the "lost city of the Incas"?

Machu Picchu was an Inca town. The town was abandoned after 1532, when the Spaniards invaded the Andes. In 1911, it was discovered by an American explorer named Hiram Bingham and became known as the "lost city of the Incas."

Around 50 miles (80 kilometers) north of Cuzco, Machu Picchu lies hidden in the jungle mountains that are at a lower altitude than Cuzco. It is about 8,000 feet (2,430 meters) above sea level. Historians think that it was built around 1440 by Sapa Inca Pachacuti, who used it when he wanted to get away from Cuzco. It was also near an important trade route between Cuzco and the jungle.

Machu Picchu sat beneath a mountain peak called Huayna Picchu and followed a long and narrow layout along the mountain ridge.

STONE OF THE SUN

At the highest point of Machu Picchu stands the Intihuatana, which means "the place where the sun is tied." This is a stone block carved out of the granite rock, and some historians think that it may have been used as a kind of sundial. However, other historians think that it represents a mountain peak. Incas thought mountains were holy and powerful and worshipped them.

Some of the buildings were set into the mountain rock, and others were built on raised stone terraces. The Incas built canals to channel water into the town from nearby mountain springs.

How was the town arranged?

Important buildings were at the top of the ridge, around a central square. Over 3,000 steps led down from here past houses for farmers, laborers, and craftworkers. Outside the town walls, there were terraces for farming and barracks for soldiers, as well as burial caves on the eastern side of the mountain.

What Was Inca Life Like?

The Inca Empire was ruled from the capital city of Cuzco. Life for many Incas was based around farming, religion, and family. Groups that the Incas conquered were allowed to keep some of their own customs and religions, as long as they agreed to worship the Sun God and to be ruled by the Sapa Inca.

 The Sapa Inca was the ruler of the whole civilization. This is a painting of Sapa Inca Atahualpa.

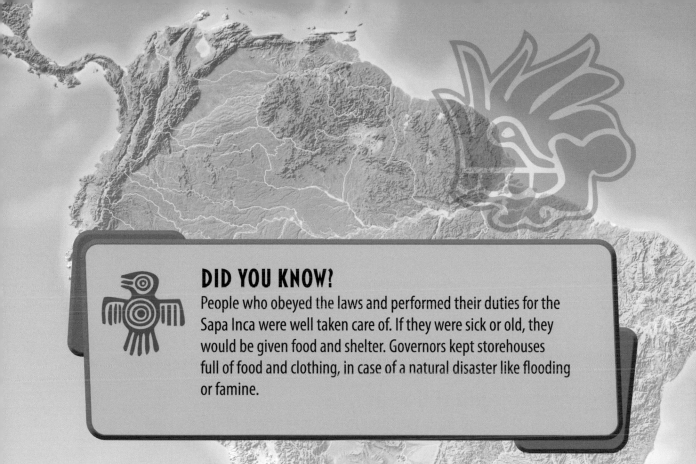

How did the leaders run the empire?

The Sapa Inca was the supreme leader. He was helped by four council leaders, one for each of the four quarters of the empire. Each quarter was split into smaller areas, or **provinces**, and each province had a capital city where the governor of that province lived. Governors had various officials to help them run their provinces and make sure the people kept to the Inca laws. People breaking the laws were punished harshly.

What were *mitimaes*?

Often whole communities in the Inca Empire were moved into newly conquered areas. These groups, called *mitimaes*, were given land there and told never to return to their homelands. This helped to spread the Inca way of life and Inca knowledge throughout the empire. It also helped to keep the newly conquered tribes under control. Officials would carry out regular **censuses** to check where people were living throughout the empire.

Which gods did the Incas worship?

For many Incas, the Sun God was the most important god. Incas believed that on Earth, the Sapa Inca represented the sun, and his wife, the Coya Inca, represented the moon. Incas thought that the stars were the children of the sun and the moon. Some **constellations** were thought to watch over certain things on Earth. For example, the Pleiades watched over farming.

Incas lived among the mountains, and this influenced their religion. They worshipped high mountains as gods. They carved huge steps, platforms, and strange shapes into natural features such as giant boulders. They made these sacred religious sites out of their dramatic landscapes.

DID YOU KNOW?

Incas made **sacrifices** to their gods to keep them happy and to prevent natural disasters such as earthquakes. Often these offerings were made at places called *huacas*. Some *huacas* were human-made, but most were natural features like mountains, springs, and caves.

This is Huaca de la Luna, which the Incas built at the base of a volcano called Cerro Blanco.

What jobs did Incas do?

Most Inca people were farmers or herders. Some were soldiers, and some worked in mines and quarries. Men had to take part in building projects for the Sapa Inca, while women tended to their homes—cooking, caring for children, working on their farms, and spinning and weaving wool.

Some Incas worked as skilled architects, engineers, and stonemasons to create buildings and roads. Craftworkers made jewelry, wood carvings, and pottery.

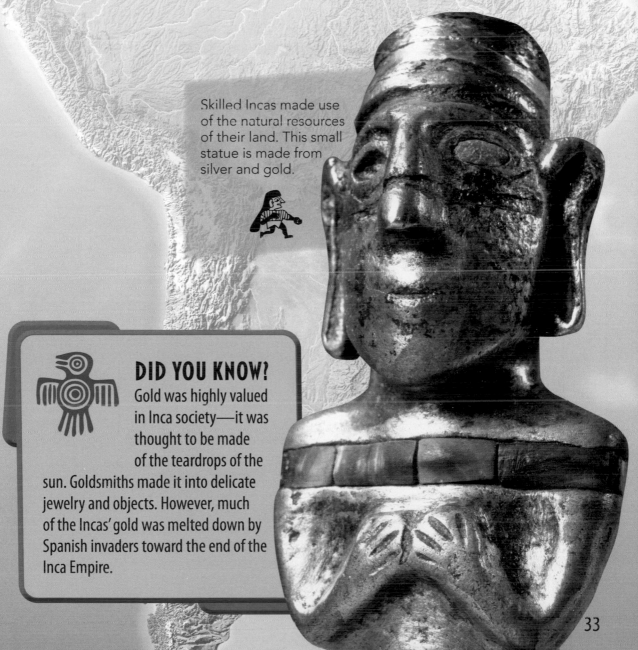

Skilled Incas made use of the natural resources of their land. This small statue is made from silver and gold.

DID YOU KNOW?

Gold was highly valued in Inca society—it was thought to be made of the teardrops of the sun. Goldsmiths made it into delicate jewelry and objects. However, much of the Incas' gold was melted down by Spanish invaders toward the end of the Inca Empire.

What scientific knowledge did the Incas have?

Inca priests studied **astronomy**. They noticed the movements of the planets around the sun, and they knew how constellations moved. They used these movements to make predictions about the seasons and weather conditions.

Yearly calendars were created by noting the position of the sun, the moon, and the stars. Incas built stone towers to calculate the changing position of the sun. Because the Incas used the phases of the moon to divide the year, the Inca year had 12 months like ours.

Incas liked to preserve the bodies of the dead. The cold, dry air in the mountains was ideal for this.

This woman is holding a ball of dyed yarn (left), made that color by the cochineal insect. On the right is a ball made of thousands of the crushed insects.

Inca medicine was a mix of magic and science. Some illnesses were thought to be caused by evil spirits. Incas sacrificed animals to help sick and injured people. However, Incas also used medicines made from local plants and from minerals such as clay.

Incas also used plants to make colored dyes for their cloth. Tiny plants called lichens gave green and brown colors, and indigo plants gave a deep-blue color. Some dried insects gave a bright-red color.

How did the Incas use their climate?

Many Inca burial sites are in cold, dry places. These provide good conditions for preserving dead bodies as mummies. The dead bodies were wrapped in layers of cloth and put into cold, dry tombs.

How Did the Inca Empire Come to an End?

Even though the Inca civilization was very successful and the empire was well organized, it lasted only a very short time. It began to collapse about 100 years after it had reached its largest size.

What happened in 1532?

Between 1525 and 1532, there was civil war in the Inca Empire as the two sons of Sapa Inca Huayna Capac—Huascar and Atahualpa—fought for power. Huayna Capac, his oldest son, and thousands of others had died of disease before this. The disease was probably smallpox, brought by the Spanish.

In 1532, Atahualpa defeated Huascar and became Sapa Inca. Later that year, a Spaniard named Francisco Pizarro arrived in the north of the Inca Empire, with around 160 soldiers. An invitation was sent from the Sapa Inca, asking Pizarro to meet him in the town of Cajamarca.

DID YOU KNOW?

Christopher Columbus had become the first European person to sail to the Americas, in 1492. News of the "New World" that he found spread through Europe, and lots of explorers followed. Many went looking for treasures such as gold. These explorers brought European diseases such as smallpox to the area.

What happened in Cajamarca?

Although there were only 160 Spanish soldiers, compared with 5,000 Inca soldiers, the Incas were defeated. The Spaniards were armed with guns and swords, while most of the Incas were less well armed. Atahualpa was captured, and his nobles and thousands of Inca soldiers were killed.

This painting shows what the capture of Atahualpa at the battle of Cajamarca might have looked like.

What happened to the Inca Empire?

In 1533, the Spanish invaders killed Atahualpa. They chose his half-brother, Manco Inca, to become the Sapa Inca. They wanted to control the Inca Empire through Manco Inca. Over the following two years, the Spanish invaders went all over the Inca Empire, stealing treasures and destroying temples and palaces. The Inca Empire began to crumble, and Manco Inca fled out of Cuzco and into the jungle.

Manco Inca fled from Cuzco into the jungle, eventually settling at a place called Vilcabanba, near Machu Picchu, shown here.

DID YOU KNOW?

Atahualpa had offered to fill rooms with gold and silver in exchange for being set free by the Spanish invaders. Gold, silver, and other treasures were sent from all around the empire. However, the Spanish killed Atahualpa instead and melted down most of the gold and silver. This was then sent back to Spain, leaving behind very few Inca treasures.

Who was the last Inca leader?

Manco Inca, his three sons, and his followers held out against the Spanish invaders for almost 40 more years. They created a small Inca stronghold around Vilcabamba, near Machu Picchu. Meanwhile, the Spaniards destroyed Inca temples and built Christian churches. They introduced Spanish customs and ways of life. Diseases such as measles, smallpox, and influenza spread among the Incas and famine became common. Thousands of Incas died.

The last group of Incas holding out at Vilcabamba were ruled by Tupac Amaru I. In 1572, he was finally defeated and executed. Inca rule was finished forever, and the Spanish went on to create a huge empire in South and Central America.

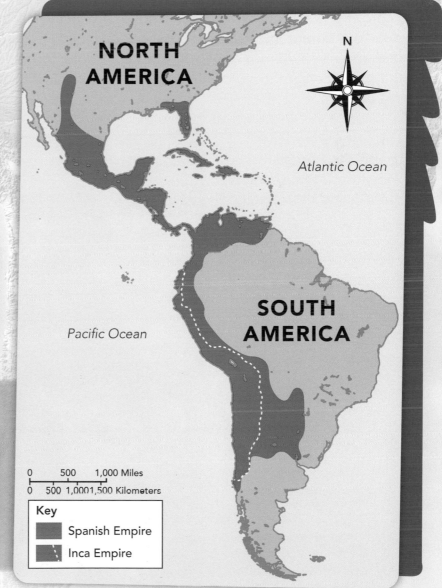

This map shows the land that the Spanish invaders had conquered by 1600. The new Spanish Empire included all of the Inca Empire.

NORTH AMERICA

N

Atlantic Ocean

Pacific Ocean

SOUTH AMERICA

| 0 | 500 | 1,000 Miles |
| 0 | 500 1,0001,500 Kilometers |

Key

Spanish Empire

Inca Empire

Was Geography Important in the Inca Empire?

A large part of Inca life was affected by the geography of the area. It helped the Incas conquer other peoples. The difficult terrain meant that small communities were isolated from each other and could not join together to fight back against the Incas.

In order to keep control of their empire, the Incas had to develop excellent **communications**. The network of roads and bridges meant that armies could move around quickly. The messenger system meant that the rulers in Cuzco could keep in close touch with all parts of the empire.

The Incas were able to use their great knowledge of farming to grow crops successfully around the empire. The land and climate varied enormously across the empire, meaning that a huge range of crops could be farmed, and famine was avoided.

The Incas grew lots of different types of one crop, such as potatoes. This meant that if one type was affected by disease, the Incas would not starve, since they could still eat the other types.

DID YOU KNOW?

Historians estimate that the gold, silver, and treasures collected to pay for Atahualpa's freedom would be worth many millions of dollars in today's money. All of this wealth was divided among the Spanish conquerors, and much of it was shipped to Spain.

Although there were many geographical obstacles to be overcome when the Incas were conquering new land, the Incas had the skills to do this. They built roads, bridges, canals, and reservoirs, for example, using technology to suit the environment. The engineering and building knowledge was so advanced that natural disasters like earthquakes had little effect on their buildings.

Because Inca society was so well organized, Inca ways of life, customs, and knowledge were quickly spread all around the empire, and this helped to create a strong civilization.

The incredible building techniques used by the Incas mean that there are many structures still standing for people to visit today.

Quiz

1

On which continent was the Inca Empire?

a) Europe

b) South America

c) Africa

2

Which mountain range was part of the Inca Empire?

a) The Andes

b) The Alps

c) The Karakoram

3

Which ocean did the Inca Empire have a coast along?

a) The Atlantic Ocean

b) The Arctic Ocean

c) The Pacific Ocean

4

Where did the Inca civilization start from?

a) The Gold Coast

b) The Cuzco Valley

c) Lake Titicaca

5

What did terraces help the Incas to overcome?

a) Steep slopes

b) Marshy land

c) High winds

6

How did Incas store food?

a) By freeze-drying it

b) Underwater

c) By salting it

7

How many miles/ kilometers of roads did the Incas build?

a) Over 150 miles (240 kilometers)

b) Over 1,500 miles (2,400 kilometers)

c) Over 15,000 miles (24,000 kilometers)

8

Which metal did Incas call "teardrops of the sun"?

a) Silver

b) Gold

c) Platinum

9

How many months did the Inca calendar have?

a) 12

b) 6

c) 24

10

Which vegetable did the Incas grow over 200 different kinds of?

a) Tomatoes

b) Wheat

c) Potatoes

11

Which animals gave the finest wool?

a) Llamas

b) Alpacas

c) Vicuñas

12

How far could a message travel through the empire in one day?

a) 200 miles (320 kilometers)

b) 130 miles (220 kilometers)

c) 75 miles (120 kilometers)

Glossary

adobe building material made of clay or mud that is mixed with straw, formed into bricks, and left to dry in the sun

altitude height above sea level

archaeologist person who studies objects from history to understand past lives

architect person who designs buildings

astronomy study of stars and planets

barren not able to produce or support living things

BCE short for "Before the Common Era," relating to dates before the birth of Jesus Christ

CE short for the "Common Era," relating to dates after the birth of Jesus Christ

census official count of the number of people living in a certain place

civilization society that has reached a high level of organization and culture

communications in geography, communications means the ways of connecting people and includes roads and sea routes as well as exchanging messages

constellation group of stars that people can identify in the sky

continent one of Earth's seven large areas of land

culture language, ideas, inventions, traditions, and art of a group of people

empire group of countries or people ruled over by a powerful leader or government

erode wear away

fertile able to produce and support plants such as farm crops

fertilizer chemicals put on land to make it fertile, allowing crops to grow better

foothills smaller hills at the bases of large mountains

fortress large building that has defenses to keep out attackers

gorge deep, narrow valley

humid   air that has lots of moisture in it

infertile   not able to produce and support plants such as farm crops

labor tax   amount of work that you have to do for people in power

litter   platform with a seat on it that was carried by people

mineral   substance in Earth that does not come from an animal or a plant

mortar   material made from lime, sand, and water that is used to hold bricks or stones in place

mummy   dead body that is preserved with special chemicals and wrapped in cloth or dried out

noble   high-ranking person

plains   large, flat area of land

province   area of a country or empire that has its own local rulers

reservoir   place where water is collected and stored

sacrifice   gift, sometimes an animal or a person, offered to a god

terrace   section of ground on a slope that is raised on one side to create a flat surface

terrain   natural shape and characteristics of the land

thatch   dried plant material, such as straw or palm leaves, that is used to cover the roofs of houses

valley   long area of low land between mountains or hills

vine   plant with a long, thin, woody stem that climbs up another plant or structure or grows along the ground

Find Out More

Books

Henty, G. A. *The Treasures of the Incas: A Story of Adventure in Peru.* Champaign, Ill.: Book Jungle, 2007 (originally published in 1903).

Koponen, Libby. *South America* (True Book). New York City: Children's Press, 2009.

Kovacs, Lawrence G. *Inca: Discover the Culture and Geography of a Lost Civilization* (Build It Yourself). White River Junction, Vt.: Nomad, 2013.

Place to Visit

The Field Museum, Chicago, Illinois
www.fieldmuseum.org
This museum's collection contains amazing artifacts from the
Inca Empire.

Tips For Further Research

El Niño
See if you can find out about El Niño—an event that affects the Pacific
Ocean off the coast of South America. Can you find any evidence of an
El Niño event during the time of the Incas?

Desert causes
Do some research to find out why the desert along the Pacific Coast in
South America is so dry. The Andes play a part in this, as they affect the
rainfall. The Pacific Ocean also helps to keep the desert very dry. See
if you can find out why.

Killer diseases
Smallpox was one of the diseases that invaders from Europe brought to
the Americas. It probably killed millions of American Indians. Do some
research to find out about the disease. Why did it kill so many American
Indians? Does it still exist today?

Index

adobe bricks 25, 27
alpaca 17
Amazon 8
Andes 5, 6, 8, 10, 28
animals 10, 17, 20, 21, 22, 35
armies 4, 20, 23, 29
astronomy 34
Atahualpa 30, 36, 37, 38

Bingham, Hiram 28
bridges 19, 40
building materials 24–25, 27
burial 29, 35

calendars 34
censuses 31
Chavin civilization 5, 6
Chimu civilization 5, 6
civil war 36
climate 5, 9, 35
Columbus, Christopher 36
communications 20–21, 40
craftworkers 33
crops 16, 40
Cuzco 20, 26, 30
Cuzco Valley 6, 10

deserts 8, 9, 12, 19
drought 9
dyes 35

earthquakes 25, 32
empire, expansion of 6, 10

farming 6, 8, 9, 12–17, 32, 40
fire beacons 20
food 15, 17
food preservation and storage 9, 15, 31

gold and silver 33, 36, 38, 41
government 31
guano 12
guinea pigs 17

homes 25, 27, 29
huacas 32
Huascar 36
Huayna Capac 10, 36

Inca civilization, beginnings of 6
Inca civilization, end of 36–39

jobs 23, 33

labor tax 23
landscapes 4, 8, 32
laws 31
litters 20
llamas 17, 20, 21, 22

Machu Picchu 4, 28–29
Manco Inca 38, 39
maps 6, 9, 10, 18, 26, 39
medicine 35
messengers 20, 21, 40
mineral resources 10, 33
mitimaes 31
Mochica civilization 5, 6
mountains 5, 6, 8, 9, 10, 12, 13, 15, 19, 27, 28, 29, 32
mummies 7, 34, 35

Nazca civilization 5, 6
Nazca lines 5
nobles 20, 26, 37

Pachacuti 6, 10, 28
pack animals 17, 20, 21

Pizarro, Francisco 36
plains 8, 12
potatoes 16, 40
provinces 31

Quechua language 6
quinoa 16

rafts 20
rain forest 8, 9, 11
religion 22, 23, 26, 30, 32
reservoirs 14
roads 18–19, 40

sacrifices 32, 35
Sacsayhuaman 26
Sapa Inca 6, 10, 22, 23, 26, 28, 30, 31, 32, 33, 36, 38
smallpox 36, 39
Spanish invaders 6, 28, 33, 36–39, 41
stone 24, 25
Sun God 22, 23, 26, 30, 32

taxes 10, 23
temples 22, 23, 26, 39
terraces 13, 15, 29
Topa Inca 10, 11
towns, cities and villages 4, 24–29
trade 22, 23, 28
travel 18–21
Tupac Amaru I 39

vicuñas 17
Vilcabamba 38, 39

water management 14, 29
women 33
writing 7